NEW ENGLAND

A PICTURE BOOK TO REMEMBER HER BY

Designed by
DAVID GIBBON

Produced by
TED SMART

CRESCENT

INTRODUCTION

New England is a region in the northeast part of America, comprising the states of Maine, Vermont, New Hampshire, Massachusetts, Rhode Island and Connecticut, which was named by Captain John Smith, an early English explorer, and a representative of certain London merchants. The following extract was quoted by the Captain on his settling in the area:–

"It is not a worke for everyone to manage such an affaire as makes a discoverie and plant a colony. It requires all the best parts of Art, Judgement, Courage, Honesty and Constancy, Diligence and Industrie to doe but neere well."

Who better to fill these requirements than the Pilgrim Fathers, who landed near present-day Provincetown, Mass, in 1620, in search of a more meaningful life.

Their famous voyage on the Mayflower, subsidized by a loan of £7,000, was later redeemed by the sale of furs from Maine's beaver dams. After signing the Mayflower Compact, they crossed the bay and founded the Plymouth Plantation. Soon more Puritans arrived, having escaped religious persecution in England, and within four years 10,000 had settled in Massachusetts. By the end of the century there were 80,000 and 50,000 more had made their homes in Rhode Island, Connecticut and New Hampshire.

They worked hard under difficult conditions, dedicating themselves to God, yet their religious fervour was, at times, more oppressive and intolerant than the society from which they had fled. Their importance in America's history, however, is significant, for they and their descendants provided many of the nation's leaders, statesmen, writers and merchants and, in addition, they established many universities and banking institutions.

The area in which the colonists settled was heavily forested, with numerous streams and rivers, the rugged coastline of which provided good, sheltered harbours. Some of the forest was cleared for farming and the timber sustained a flourishing shipbuilding industry. Saw and grist mills were constructed and fishing and fur-trading were also important.

During the 18th century the colonists, discontented with the actions of the British Government, agitated for independence. The attempt by the British to levy a tax on tea led to the notorious Boston Tea Party of 1773, when citizens disguised as Red Indians boarded ships carrying tea and threw it into the harbour. This incident was just one of many events which helped to spark the Revolutionary War.

After the War New England's policy of reform, particularly on the anti-slavery issue, was a major factor in the events leading to the Civil War; New England staunchly supporting the cause of the Union. The close of the Civil War, in 1865, saw a flood of immigrants, including Irish famine workers, Lithuanians, Jews, Italians and Portuguese into the North East. With the establishment of new patterns of culture by these ethnic groups New England lost its rural character but gained, instead, an enormous and skilled labour force that would prove invaluable in the Industrial Revolution of the 19th century.

In the 20th century New England remains a successful manufacturing region, the emphasis placed on producing goods of high quality and small bulk. The area is also renowned for its higher educational institutions such as Harvard in Massachusetts, founded in 1635 and Yale in Connecticut, which dates back to 1701.

Massachusetts, with a landscape dotted by lakes and rivers, is famed for its ocean resorts, lovely old towns and the famous vacation islands of Nantucket and Martha's Vineyard. The 65 mile-long Cape Cod is noted for its Cod Fisheries with treacherous off-shore waters. Since the early 1640's, when John Winthrop established a salt and ironworks, the State has been a noted manufacturing area and today, watches, shoes and paper are amongst its most important products.

Rhode Island, the smallest state of the U.S., was founded in 1636 by Roger Williams, who had been exiled from the Massachusetts Bay Colony for religious dissent. Although two-thirds of the Island is uncultivated woodland, where land has been cleared dairy and poultry farming, particularly of the world-famous Rhode Islands Reds, are carried out. Market gardening, and fishing along the coast are also important to the State's economy.

West of Rhode Island is Connecticut, a state that still preserves its colonial traditions despite its being primarily an industrial area. Eli Whitney, one of its citizens, was the celebrated inventor of the cotton gin, who introduced the principle of mass-production. Today the manufacture of helicopters, submarines, aircraft engines and ammunition play a vital role in the state's economy, whilst its close proximity to New York has led to the development of large and prosperous suburban communities.

Mountains are the most striking feature of the New Hampshire countryside, and the first American ski-school was established in this beautiful state, known as the 'Granite State' because of its stone quarries. Forest trails, lakes and rivers attract numerous visitors, and the board and batten and clapboard houses are a familiar sight whether painted white or New England barn-red, a colour derived from the early settlers' use of ox-blood.

Vermont is a major producer of timber, pulp, granite and marble, the latter being used in the construction of the Supreme Court Building in Washington D.C. and the United Nations Headquarters in New York City. Tourism is vitally important to this lovely state and is an important contribution to the economy.

Maine's rugged coastline, with over 2,000 off-shore islands, is a favourite retreat of holiday-makers. Delicious lobsters, apples and blueberries are internationally famous. The chief occupation of the state is logging as eighty per cent of the inland area is covered by forest, and although the largest of the New England States it is the most sparsely populated east of the Mississippi River; its slow economic growth resulting in the preservation of much of its magnificent landscape.

Against the rich colours of a Vermont fall *left* flutters the 'Star Spangled Banner'.

Silhouetted in the soft light of the setting sun *overleaf*, the Bass Harbour Head Light is set in the cliffs of the Acadia National Park in Maine.

A rugged coastline punctuated by white-washed lighthouses *left* is part of the characteristic charm of Maine, the largest of the New England states, and the Acadia National Park incorporates a series of beautiful inlets and coves, among them Seal Harbour *below* and Boothbay Harbour *above and overleaf*, the unspoilt centre of a busy resort area. In the same park, Fort Edgcomb *right*, a vestige of the 1812 war is now a much visited historic site.

Bar Harbour *below* with its array of lobster traps became a fashionable resort in the 1880s but in 1947 a devastating fire destroyed many of its fine buildings and despite its great natural beauty, its popularity waned.

The picturesque bay *below left* is part of the landscape around Belfast and farther inland are the leafy woodlands *left* and weather-boarded houses *above and right* for which Maine is renowned.

Boating and fishing are two of the state's most popular pastimes. The Demariscotta River *above left* is famous for the running of the alewives, a fish unique to America and *overleaf* sailing boats and pleasure cruisers lie at their tranquil moorings in Northeast Harbour.

Maine's attractive wooden buildings *above left* and its extensive forests *above* mean that the possibility of fire is an ever-present hazard. Woodland makes up 80% of the state, the remainder may be said to revolve round the sea as a source of pleasure and a means of earning a living. Deer Isle *left* provided inspiration for John Steinbeck's book 'Travels with Charley', Owl's Head *below left* is a charming secluded harbour and Camden *below and below right* is one of Maine's most popular resorts. In Stonington *above right*, lobster catchers prepare for the day's work. *Overleaf*, a house in Blue Hill village nestles among the russet-coloured Autumn foliage.

Near Deer Isle, Blue Hill village, with its restaurant decorated with colourful window-boxes *above*, is characteristic of Maine's smaller settlements, in wooded settings *left* dappled by the rays of the New England sun.

Camden River's waterfalls *below* run beneath the main street in Camden and cascade into the harbour *below right*, from which graceful schooners sail the Maine coast.

The city of Bath has a tradition of shipbuilding which dates back to 1607 and the launching of the 'Virginia', the first ocean going trading ship built in America. Washington Street *below left* has retained some of the gracious homes built by successful shipbuilders in the 18th century.

Although now several miles from the sea, Wiscasset *above left, above, below, right and far right* was once a seafaring town and the principal port east of Boston. Like Bath it was noted for its shipbuilding and has been carefully preserved in its picturesque setting.

Maine is the state of rugged shorelines, rough seas and tranquil inland countryside. The Portland Head Lighthouse *above*, dating back to 1791, when its construction was ordered by George Washington, still wards ships from the treacherous rocks off Portland. At Cape Elizabeth *right* dramatic cliffs rise from the ever-threatening waters of the Atlantic Ocean. In Rumford *left* a solitary house finds its reflection in the still waters of the Androscoggin River and *below* a typical white frame, single-spired New England church reaches towards a vivid blue sky.

The red and gold of autumnal leaves transform whatever they touch: *above left* a regimented row of sombre gravestones, *top* an old fire engine parked among the trees near Hanover, *above and below* the wooden houses in the lovely surrounds of Rangely and *left and right* the much-loved churches of Bethel and York.

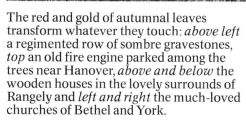

outh of Maine lies New Hampshire with
s spectacular White Mountains *right* and
ne 1,100 square miles of forest supporting a
ourishing wildlife that have made it the
aunt of hunters like those *below*. New
Hampshire has been said to encompass
ome of the finest unspoilt areas in New
ngland, exemplified here in the
ninterrupted windings of the Saco River
verleaf or the River Beebe *below right*,
panned by its distinctive covered bridge.
ear West Thornton stands the solitary
rm *above right* with its lofty red barn,
nd the Catholic Church *above* and the
ouse nestling among the trees *left* are part
Bethlehem.

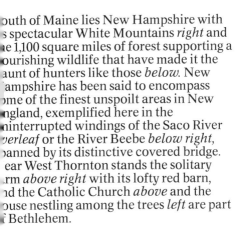

New Hampshire is very much a region tied to its past. Some of the weatherboarded buildings *above* have stood at Tufton Corner since 1795 and the names of many of its beautiful towns and lakes, like Lake Winnipesaukee *on these pages and overleaf* are picturesque reminders of the Indians who inhabited northern New England before the coming of the white man in the 17th century.

Vermont is primarily rural but into its harmony of hills, fields and forests, attractive towns and villages with a distinctive Vermont atmosphere are also blended. Woodstock *on these pages*, the home of four of Vermont's eight Paul Revere bells, has been skilfully restored to preserve its elegant eighteenth and nineteenth century buildings.

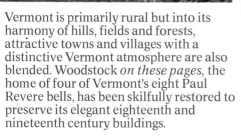

The old world atmosphere of the village stores in Marshfields *above, left and below,* reflect Vermont's desire to preserve its historical heritage. So also does Shelburne Museum, a 45 acre park containing thirty-five historic buildings brought here from all parts of the state to house a magnificent range of arts and crafts. Among the exhibits, the railway station *below left* recalls the days of the first railroad, brought to Vermont in 1848.

Set among an extension of the Appalachian Mountain system, that covers most of the 'Green Mountain State' are the breathtakingly beautiful scenes shown *right.*

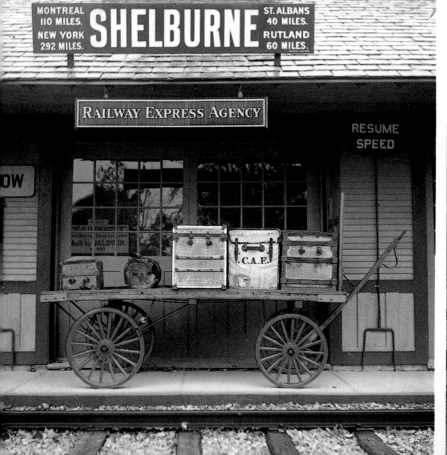

Deerfield, Massachusetts, *on these pages and overleaf* is a village specially designated as a National Historic District. Here, among the New England leaves, which in Autumn fall in their millions to form a rich russet carpet, are a number of buildings, now over 150 years old, for despite the Indian attacks, which from 1672–1704 destroyed many of the original houses, restoration has recreated a delightful village: *above and right,* Dwight Barnard House Museum, *left,* Sheldon Hawkes House and *below,* Rev. John Ashley House.

Weatherboarded and stone houses melt into the rolling pastures, woodlands and lakes near Sturbridge and Mount Tom, Massachusetts *on these pages,* and rural scenes of 18th century New England are recreated in a timeless landscape. A pair of oxen working the land with a wooden plough *below* are a nostalgic echo of the almost forgotten days before modern mechanisation.

In April, 1775 Concord, Massachusetts was the site of the first battle of the War of American Independence. Today, unspoilt by the ravages of war, it boasts many fine buildings, among them its lovely white church *above left and right*.

Nearby is the Wayside Inn at South Sudbury *above*, which first opened its doors to weary travellers nearly 280 years ago and which the poet Longfellow immortalized in his 'Tales of a Wayside Inn'.

The vestige of a bygone era, an old well *left* remains in the shade of the trees at Ipswich.

Not far from Gloucester a small working boat *below* waits in Rockport Harbour.

At the point where Charles River enters the Massachusetts Bay *overleaf* sprawls the great city of Boston, the state capital.

Boston is a city of infinite variety in which the old and the new have been perfectly harmonized. Soaring skyscrapers *above left and left* in the Back Bay rise dramatically over historical buildings like the first Church of Christ the Scientist *below left* or the State House *below* with its dome covered in pure gold. The monument *top* stands in Boston Common, America's oldest public park and the scene of numerous hangings during the city's early days. The bedroom *above* is part of a house owned by Paul Revere from 1770–1800, now the oldest standing structure in downtown Boston and the replica of H.M.S. Beaver *right* is one of the fine exhibits in the Boston Tea Party Museum.

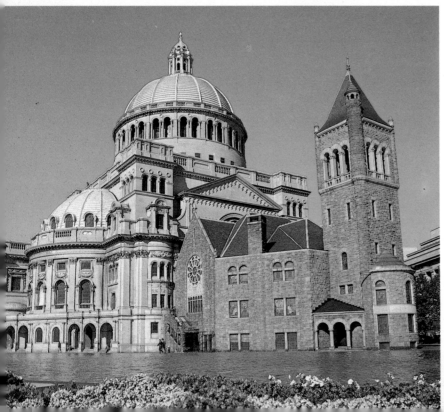

Founded in 1636, Harvard University *on this page* in Cambridge, Massachusetts is America's oldest institution of higher learning. It is named after John Harvard, a Puritan minister, who bequeathed half his estate and his library to the university and a statue on the campus *below* commemorates this act of generosity.

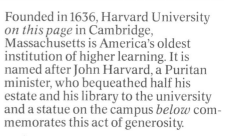

Liberty & the Rights of mankind!!!
The Freedom & Independence of America.
Sealed & defended with the blood of her sons.

This Monument is erected
By the inhabitants of Lexington,
Under the patronage, & at the expence, of
The Commonwealth of Massachusetts,
To the memory of their Fellow Citizens,
Ensign Robert Munroe, Mess.' Jonas Parker,
Samuel Hadley, Jonathan Harrington Jun.'
Isaac Muzzy, Caleb Harrington and John Brown
Of Lexington, & Asahel Porter of Woburn.
Who fell on this field, the first Victims to the
Sword of British Tyranny & Oppression,
On the morning of the ever memorable
Nineteenth of April, An. Dom. 1775.
The Die was cast!!!
The Blood of these Martyrs,
In the cause of God & their Country,
Was the Cement of the Union of these States, then
Colonies; & gave the spring to the spirit, Firmness
And resolution of their Fellow Citizens,
They rose as one man, to revenge their brethren's
Blood, and at the point of the sword, to assert &
Defend their native Rights.
They nobly dar'd to be free!!
The contest was long, bloody & affecting.
Righteous Heaven approved the solemn appeal;
Victory crowned their arms; and
The Peace, Liberty & Independence of the United
States of America, was their glorious Reward.
Built in the year 1799.

Northwest of Boston is the attractive suburb of Lexington, with its charming secluded church *below right*. It was here that as the plaque *above* relates, on April 19th, 1755, seventy-seven Minutemen stood against seven hundred British soldiers and lost eight of their number in the opening skirmish of the Revolutionary War. Still standing on the Green are many of the original buildings and a statue *right* of Captain John Parker, who commanded the Minutemen, pays tribute to the courage that made Lexington 'The Birthplace of American Liberty'.

Many notorious trials for witchcraft were carried out in Salem, Massachusetts in the late seventeenth century. Those times have long gone but many of the buildings dating from that period have been restored like the one *below* and are on view to the public.

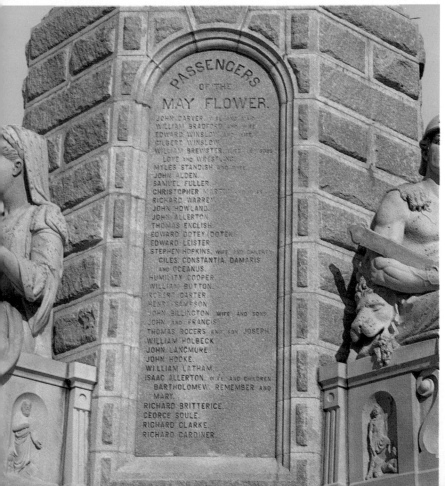

PASSENGERS
OF THE
MAY FLOWER.

JOHN CARVER, WIFE AND MAID
WILLIAM BRADFORD AND WIFE
EDWARD WINSLOW AND WIFE
GILBERT WINSLOW
WILLIAM BREWSTER, WIFE LOVE AND WRESTLING
LOVE AND WRESTLING
MYLES STANDISH AND WIFE
JOHN ALDEN.
SAMUEL FULLER.
CHRISTOPHER MARTIN AND WIFE
RICHARD WARREN.
JOHN HOWLAND.
JOHN ALLERTON.
THOMAS ENGLISH.
EDWARD DOTEY (DOTEN)
EDWARD LEISTER.
STEPHEN HOPKINS, WIFE AND CHILDREN
GILES, CONSTANTIA, DAMARIS
AND OCEANUS.
HUMILITY COOPER.
WILLIAM BUTTON.
ROBERT CARTER.
HENRY SAMPSON.
JOHN BILLINGTON, WIFE AND SONS
JOHN AND FRANCIS.
THOMAS ROGERS AND SON JOSEPH.
WILLIAM HOLBECK.
JOHN LANGMORE.
JOHN HOOKE.
WILLIAM LATHAM.
ISAAC ALLERTON, WIFE AND CHILDREN
BARTHOLOMEW, REMEMBER AND
MARY.
RICHARD BRITTERICE.
GEORGE SOULE.
RICHARD CLARKE.
RICHARD GARDINER.

It was in Plymouth, Massachusetts, that the weary Pilgrims landed in December 1620 in their small ship, the 'Mayflower'. A monument *left and below* lists the courageous passengers on board, half of whom survived the journey, only to lose their lives during their first harsh winter in America. 'Mayflower II' *above* is an impressive replica of the original ship that made the momentous crossing.

Red and golden foliage frames a lovely house in Duxbury *right*.

Cape Cod was first discovered in 1602 by an English navigator, Bartholomew Gosnold, who named it after the large shoals of cod he found there. Today its rolling sand dunes *below right,* and its great natural beauty studded with picturesque buildings like the Eastham windmill *above,* or the dazzling white lighthouses of Chatham *above right* and Provincetown *below,* have made it a popular tourist resort. Historically Provincetown, with its McMillan Wharf above left, is the point where the Pilgrims first landed before continuing to Plymouth.

Despite the appeal it holds for tourists, the miles of varied Massachusetts coastline have remained largely unspoilt. Sunset *left* bathes Buzzards Bay in golden light and pleasure boats *right* are mirrored in the sheltered waters of Mychmere Harbour.

Rhode Island, although the smallest state in the nation, is a state of compact variety, of woodland *below* and farmland *below far right*, of busy fishing ports *right*, slender lighthouses *below right* and gracious country houses *far right* that have stood since colonial days.

Providence, the state capital, is an important deep water port and commercial centre in which the modern skyline of downtown *below left* contrasts vividly with the city's greatest historical legacy… the beautiful white Georgian marble State Capitol *centre left*. The County Court *above left* was constructed in 1933 and the church *above* forms part of old Providence.

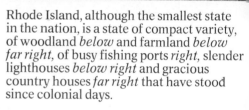

Rolling hills and tree-filled valleys stamped with attractive towns and villages are the mark of the state of Connecticut and the setting for the Charles Goodwin Dam *above right* and the lovely old farmstead at Newgate *below right*.

Hartford, the state capital and largest city, is the home of many major insurance companies and towering buildings, which at night cast their glittering reflections on the waters of the Connecticut River *above*. The gold-domed Capitol *above left*, once described as a 'Gothic Taj Mahal', sits dramatically on the highest point in Bushnell Park. Nook Farm *below left* was the grand Victorian home of Mark Twain from 1874-1891.

The white steepled Congregational Church *below* dominates Litchfield Green.

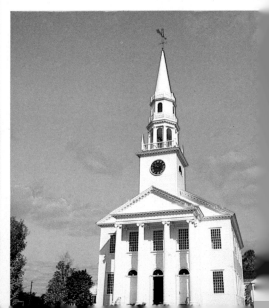

New Haven, Connecticut's third city, is famous above all for Yale University *on these pages*, the third oldest university in the United States. Founded in 1701, it was named after Elihu Yale, one-time governor of Fort St. George, Madras, who in 1718 made a substantial donation to what was then a college. As an institution of higher learning it acquired university status in 1887 and in 1969 these beautiful old buildings first opened their doors to admit women.

Connecticut represents a special blending of modern urban life with a deep sense of its history and its environment... crystal clear rivers and lakes *left*, quiet village greens surrounded by gracious homes like the one *below* in Cheshire or the old stone house at Guildford *right*, and golden beaches and peaceful harbours. Mystic Seaport *above and overleaf* is a vivid reflection of a desire to preserve the best of the past, for with its reconstructed buildings and old ships it is an exact replica of a typical seafaring village of the early nineteenth century.

First published in Great Britain 1979 by Colour Library International Ltd.
© Illustrations: Colour Library International Ltd, 163 East 64th Street, New York 10021.
Colour separations by Fercrom, Barcelona, Spain.
Display and text filmsetting by Focus Photoset, London, England.
Printed by CEDAG, S. A. bound by EUROBINDER - Barcelona-Spain
Published by Crescent Books, a division of Crown Publishers Inc.
Library of Congress Catalogue Card No. 78-74855
CRESCENT 1979

Dep. leg.: B. 18.531/1980